TOMBSTONES
Final Resting Places of the Famous

GREGG FELSEN

Andrews McMeel
Publishing

Kansas City

www.andrewsmcmeel.com

ISBN: 0-7407-0081-2

Library of Congress Catalog Card Number: 99-72684

Design by Holly Camerlinck

This book is dedicated to my father, Arthur Felsen, who, like many of the famous men and women in this book, overcame many obstacles on his way to success. He has been a supportive and compassionate friend as well as a loving father and grandfather.

INTRODUCTION

As a photographer, writer, and someone who has always been interested in the lives, achievements, triumphs over adversity, and deaths of famous people, exploring cemeteries has been a passion of mine for thirty years. During that time I have recorded on film the final resting places of more than three hundred world-famous writers, artists, musicians, entertainers, sports legends, scientists and inventors, government and business leaders, colonists and patriots, social reformers, folk heroes, and cultural icons.

I have traveled frequently and extensively throughout Europe and North America. My journeys have taken me to hundreds of cemeteries including small village churchyards, picturesque garden cemeteries, military cemeteries, and large modern memorial parks. Places of haunting beauty, tranquillity, and history, cemeteries are more than necropolises of statuaries. They are places for quiet reflection and meditation, and the memorials within them represent personal expressions of love and respect for the departed. They celebrate life and focus on immortality rather than mortality.

Long after the deaths of such famous public figures as Frédéric Chopin, Marie Curie, James Dean, Martin Luther King Jr., Abraham Lincoln, Mickey Mantle, Marilyn Monroe, Elvis Presley, Frank Sinatra, Vincent van Gogh,

Jules Verne, and many more, their grave sites remain meccas for fans, admirers, and cemetery tourists like myself wishing to pay their respects and to discover for themselves the various ways in which these influential and talented men and women have been memorialized.

When I stand at the grave sites of so many world-famous individuals, I feel a genuine sense of communion and connectedness with them. Far from ghoulish or morbid, touring cemeteries for me has been a highly educational, rewarding, and respectable pastime. Through this book, I am pleased to share forty-four of my favorite images with all fellow and future cemetery tourists.

SUSAN B. ANTHONY

BORN: February 15, 1820, in Adams, Massachusetts

DIED: March 15, 1906, in Rochester, New York

BURIED: Mount Hope Cemetery in Rochester, New York

CONTRIBUTION: Relentless reformer, advocate, and early leader of women's suffrage movement, abolitionist who campaigned for emancipation of slaves; cofounder of National Woman Suffrage Association (1869) and president of National American Suffrage Association (1892–1900). Her fifty years of work helped pave the way for the passage of the Nineteenth Amendment to the Constitution, which gave women in America the right to vote.

CAUSE OF DEATH: Heart failure induced by pneumonia of both lungs

LUCILLE BALL

BORN: August 6, 1911, in Jamestown, New York

DIED: April 26, 1989, in Los Angeles, California

BURIED: Forest Lawn Memorial Park in Hollywood Hills, California

CONTRIBUTION: Screen actress who appeared in more than sixty films in the 1930s and 1940s; queen of TV comedy for twenty-five years and best known as the Emmy-winning star of *I Love Lucy*, which premiered on October 15, 1951, and was broadcast in prime time until June 1957. Ball also starred in 156 episodes of *The Lucy Show* (1962–1968) and 144 episodes of *Here's Lucy* (1968–1972). She was an astute businesswoman who headed her own studio, Desilu Productions.

CAUSE OF DEATH: Bled to death following the rupture of her abdominal aorta one week after undergoing a seven-hour emergency open-heart surgery to replace a tear in her aorta and a damaged aortic valve

SARAH BERNHARDT

BORN: October 22, 1844, in Paris, France

DIED: March 26, 1923, in Paris, France

BURIED: Père Lachaise Cemetery in Paris, France

CONTRIBUTION: Celebrated French stage tragedienne; international superstar who performed throughout the world for sixty years. Known as "The Divine Sarah," she was famous for her larger-than-life personality and her extravagant lifestyle. Hers is the face that appears on dozens of Mucha art nouveau posters that are still popular today.

CAUSE OF DEATH: Acute uremia

DANIEL BOONE

DANIEL BOONE

BORN: November 2, 1734, in Berks County, Pennsylvania

DIED: September 26, 1820, in St. Charles, Missouri

BURIED: Frankfort Cemetery in Frankfort, Kentucky

CONTRIBUTION: Adventurous trapper, hunter, backwoodsman, and wilderness guide; first hero of the westward movement in America; a legendary symbol of the early American frontier. Boone led settlers overland from North Carolina to explore and settle new territories on the ever-expanding western frontier during the last half of the eighteenth century.

CAUSE OF DEATH: Acute indigestion and unknown causes following a large meal of sweet potatoes at the home of his son five days before Boone's eighty-sixth birthday

JOHN WILKES BOOTH

BORN: May 10, 1838, near Bel Air, Maryland

DIED: April 26, 1865, near Port Royal, Virginia

BURIED: Green Mount Cemetery in Baltimore, Maryland

CONTRIBUTION: Handsome, well-educated stage actor and celebrity; Southern sympathizer during the Civil War; lone assassin who shot President Lincoln at point-blank range at 10:15 P.M. on Good Friday, April 14, 1865, as the president was watching *Our American Cousin* at Ford's Theatre in Washington, D.C.

CAUSE OF DEATH: Shot to death by cavalrymen while hiding from authorities inside a tobacco shed on the farm of Richard Garrett, who was unaware of Booth's identity or his role in the assassination of Lincoln

CARPENTER

EARTH TO EARTH A YEAR OF LABOUR A GRAIN OF WHEAT

HAROLD 1949–1988 BELOVED HUSBAND DAD AND GRANDAD

AGNES 1919–1996 BELOVED WIFE MUM AND GRANDMOTHER

KAREN CARPENTER

BORN: March 2, 1950, in New Haven, Connecticut

DIED: February 4, 1983, in Downey, California

BURIED: Forest Lawn Memorial Park in Cypress, California

CONTRIBUTION: Member of three-time Grammy-winning pop duo, the Carpenters; singer of soft-rock love songs, including "Close To You" and "We've Only Just Begun," during the 1970s. With her brother, Richard, and singing his arrangements, Karen Carpenter performed at sold-out concerts throughout the country, headlined in Las Vegas, and sold seventeen million albums.

CAUSE OF DEATH: Heart failure caused by anorexia nervosa, an eating disorder primarily affecting women that is characterized by a pathological fear of gaining weight, dangerous eating patterns, and excessive weight loss. Carpenter was the first celebrity known to die from this disorder.

FRÉDÉRIC CHOPIN

BORN: February 22, 1810, in Zelazowa Wola, Poland

DIED: October 17, 1849, in Paris, France

BURIED: Père Lachaise Cemetery in Paris, France

CONTRIBUTION: Musical child prodigy; visionary and innovative Polish pianist, composer, and teacher. Chopin gave his first public concert at the age of eight and, because of an intense aversion to crowds, performed in public only thirty times in his lifetime.

CAUSE OF DEATH: Tuberculosis, which he contracted in 1835

SIDONIE COLETTE

BORN: January 28, 1873, in Saint-Saveur-en-Puisaye, Burgandy, France

DIED: August 3, 1954, in Paris, France

BURIED: Père Lachaise Cemetery in Paris, France

CONTRIBUTION: Modern French writer; an advocate of feminine independence whose more than fifty novels and scores of short stories were concerned largely with the pleasures and pains of love. Colette started Audrey Hepburn on her road to fame by selecting Hepburn to play the heroine in the stage adaptation of her famous novel *Gigi* in 1952.

CAUSE OF DEATH: Heart failure

MARIE CURIE

BORN: November 7, 1867, in Warsaw, Poland

DIED: July 4, 1934, in Sallanches, France

BURIED: Originally buried in Sceaux Cemetery in Sceaux, France, and reinterred in the Pantheon in Paris, France, in April 1995

CONTRIBUTION: Research scientist who was awarded Nobel Prizes in physics (1903), for her discovery of radioactivity, and in chemistry (1911), for her discoveries of the elements polonium and radium. After World War I, she devoted her research to the application of radioactive substances for medical purposes.

CAUSE OF DEATH: Long-term accumulated exposure to radioactivity, which resulted in numerous physical problems including leukemia

MILES DAVIS

BORN: May 25, 1926, in Alton, Illinois

DIED: September 28, 1991, in Santa Monica, California

BURIED: Woodlawn Cemetery in the Bronx, New York

CONTRIBUTION: Controversial and charismatic trend-setting trumpeter whose visionary style influenced jazz from the late 1940s to the early 1970s. Davis broadened the appeal of jazz more than any other performer of his era.

CAUSE OF DEATH: Pneumonia, respiratory failure, and a stroke after being hospitalized for several weeks

JAMES DEAN

BORN: February 8, 1931, in Marion, Indiana

DIED: September 30, 1955, near Cholame, California

BURIED: Park Cemetery in Fairmount, Indiana

CONTRIBUTION: Onetime law student turned actor who appeared in TV drama specials and on Broadway from 1952 to 1954 and who became an overnight film star and eternal popular icon. Dean, who identified with the inarticulate troubled characters he played on screen, appeared in only three movies during his lifetime, *East of Eden*, *Rebel Without a Cause*, and *Giant*, all filmed between May 1954 and September 1955.

CAUSE OF DEATH: Injuries—including a broken neck, multiple broken bones, and numerous internal injuries—sustained when the 1955 two-seater Porsch Spyder he was driving at high speed collided head-on with a 1950 Ford. Dean was en route from Los Angeles to Salinas, California, where he planned to take part in a weekend of car racing.

EMILY DICKINSON

BORN: December 10, 1830, in Amherst, Massachusetts

DIED: May 15, 1886, in Amherst, Massachusetts

BURIED: West Cemetery in Amherst, Massachusetts

CONTRIBUTION: One of the greatest poets of the nineteenth century. Dickinson led a reclusive life and was unrecognized and unappreciated during her lifetime. Her eighteen hundred poems were brief, metaphoric, often did not rhyme, had eccentric syntax, and contained intensely descriptive words. Frequent subjects were love, death, nature, and separation. Only seven of her poems were published before her death.

CAUSE OF DEATH: Bright's disease, a slow failure of the kidneys

GEORGE EASTMAN

BORN: July 12, 1854, in Waterville, New York

DIED: March 14, 1932, in Rochester, New York

BURIED: Cremated ashes rest beneath the Eastman Memorial on grounds of Kodak Park in Rochester, New York

CONTRIBUTION: Onetime $3-a-week messenger boy at an insurance company who later founded the Eastman Kodak company, which was a $200 million company by 1932. Eastman made picture taking affordable and convenient for the masses and created the transparent film that made movies a reality. Unmarried his entire life, Eastman gave away $75 million for educational, artistic, scientific, and humanitarian projects throughout his life.

CAUSE OF DEATH: Self-inflicted gunshot wound to the heart after dismissing his physician and nurse from his room and writing a note that read "Why wait, my work is done."

SIGMUND FREUD

BORN: May 6, 1856, in Freiberg, Moravia

DIED: September 23, 1939, in London, England

BURIED: Golders Green Cemetery in London, England

CONTRIBUTION: Studied and trained in the natural sciences, but found the human mind more interesting. He counseled patients for fifty years and founded a system of psychology and method of treatment known as psychoanalysis, which became one of the most controversial and influential doctrines of the twentieth century.

CAUSE OF DEATH: Several injections of morphine, requested by Freud to end his life, because of the excruciating pain from cancer of the mouth and jaw, which was diagnosed in 1923. Freud endured thirty-three operations, severe disfigurement, and a painful prosthetic device that impaired his eating, speaking, and hearing.

AUDREY HEPBURN

BORN: May 4, 1929, in Brussels, Belgium

DIED: January 20, 1993, in Tolochenaz, Switzerland

BURIED: Village Cemetery in Tolochenaz, Switzerland, overlooking Lake Geneva

CONTRIBUTION: Former Dutch ballerina turned London chorus girl and fashion model; discovered by French writer Sidonie Colette and given the starring role in the Broadway adaptation of Colette's novel *Gigi*. Hepburn epitomized Hollywood chic in the 1950s and 1960s; she made twenty-six motion pictures, including *Roman Holiday* (1954) for which she won an Oscar as Best Actress; *Sabrina* (1954); *Breakfast at Tiffany's* (1961); and *My Fair Lady* (1964). She was presented with a Screen Actors Guild Award for lifetime achievement in 1993 and served as an impassioned roving goodwill ambassador for UNICEF from 1985 until her death.

CAUSE OF DEATH: Colon cancer

JAMES BUTLER "WILD BILL" HICKOCK

BORN: May 27, 1837, in Homer (later Troy Grove), Illinois

DIED: August 2, 1876, in Deadwood, South Dakota

BURIED: Mount Moriah Cemetery in Deadwood, South Dakota

CONTRIBUTION: Cavalry scout; stagecoach driver; guide of hunting and adventure parties across the plains; Civil War veteran; peace officer; stage-show performer in "Buffalo Bill" Cody's Wild West show.

CAUSE OF DEATH: Fatal gunshot wound fired from a .45-caliber Colt to the back of the head while he was playing poker with three men at Nuttall and Mann's No. 10 Saloon. His assassin, a drifter named Jack McCall, was convicted for the shooting and hanged on March 1, 1877.

BUDDY HOLLY*

BORN: September 7, 1936, in Lubbock, Texas

DIED: February 3, 1959, near Clear Lake, Iowa

BURIED: City of Lubbock Cemetery, Lubbock, Texas

CONTRIBUTION: One of the most innovative and distinctive American rock 'n' roll singers, songwriters, and musicians of the late 1950s; influenced many future musicians; best known for two songs, "That'll Be The Day" and "Peggy Sue."

CAUSE OF DEATH: Injuries sustained in a crash of a chartered four-seat single-engine plane en route to Fargo, North Dakota, minutes after takeoff from the Mason City, Iowa, airport

* Buddy Holly's given name was Charles Hardin Holley. When he signed his first contract with Decca Records in 1956, his name was misspelled as Holly and he kept that name for the rest of his life.

HARRY HOUDINI

BORN: March 24, 1874, in Budapest, Hungary

DIED: October 31, 1926, in Detroit, Michigan

BURIED: Machpelah Cemetery in Queens, New York

CONTRIBUTION: World-renowned magician, escape artist, illusionist, and showman; author; exposer of fraudulent mediums and false claims in the field of spiritualism.

CAUSE OF DEATH: Advanced peritonitis that developed following surgery for the removal of his appendix, which had been ruptured by a McGill University college student, George Whitehead, who delivered a series of unexpected blows to Houdini's abdomen on October 22, 1926

JESSE JAMES

BORN: September 5, 1847, in Clay County, Missouri

DIED: April 3, 1882, in St. Joseph, Missouri

BURIED: Originally buried at Jesse James Farm, two miles northeast of Kearney, Missouri; reinterred at Mt. Olivet Cemetery in Kearney, Missouri, in 1902.

CONTRIBUTION: Notorious train, bank, and stagecoach robber who was never arrested; a perpetual folk hero, national celebrity, and the subject of numerous biographies, historical novels, and films because of his resistance to the injustices he felt were brought against supporters of the South during the Civil War.

CAUSE OF DEATH: Gunshot from a .45-caliber Colt to the back of his head fired from a distance of four feet by Robert Ford, a member of the James-Younger gang, who killed James for the $10,000 reward offered for his capture dead or alive

AL JOLSON

BORN: May 26, 1886, in Seredzius, Lithuania

DIED: October 23, 1950, in San Francisco, California

BURIED: Hillside Memorial Park in Los Angeles, California

CONTRIBUTION: Burlesque and vaudeville performer in early 1900s; one of the greatest Broadway and film actors, recording artists, live performers, and radio personalities of his time; one of the highest paid stars in Hollywood during the 1920s and 1930s. Best known for his starring role in *The Jazz Singer* (1927), the first successful feature film with sound, and for his blackface singing of such songs as "Swanee," "Sunnyboy," and "Mammy."

CAUSE OF DEATH: Heart attack while playing cards with friends at the St. Francis Hotel only three weeks after returning to America from a strenuous tour in Korea where he entertained American troops

JAMES JOYCE

BORN: February 2, 1882, in Dublin, Ireland

DIED: January 13, 1941, in Zurich, Switzerland

BURIED: Fluntern Cemetery in Zurich, Switzerland

CONTRIBUTION: Controversial Irish poet and writer who used complex and remote symbolism as well as "stream of consciousness" writing in his intricate novels such as *Ulysses*, which was banned in America for eleven years, and *Finnegans Wake*. He was considered an innovator of literature by some critics and a charlatan by others.

CAUSE OF DEATH: Complications from emergency surgery performed on January 11, 1941, for a perforated ulcer

MARTIN LUTHER KING JR.

BORN: January 15, 1929, in Atlanta, Georgia

DIED: April 4, 1968, in Memphis, Tennessee

BURIED: Martin Luther King Jr. National Historic Site in Atlanta, Georgia

CONTRIBUTION: Baptist minister; civil rights leader; eloquent spokesman for racial justice who espoused nonviolence and was the voice of black Americans in the 1950s and 1960s. King led the peaceful movement that ended more than a century of racial segregation, which resulted in the 1964 Civil Rights Act and the 1965 Voting Rights Act. He was named "Man of the Year" by *Time* magazine and received the Nobel Peace Prize in 1964.

CAUSE OF DEATH: Injuries from a single shot fired by an assassin from a high-powered hunting rifle. The bullet struck King in the neck and severed his spinal cord. Emergency surgery was unsuccessful.

ABRAHAM LINCOLN

BORN: February 12, 1809, three miles south of Hodgenville on the south fork of Nolin Creek in Hardin County, Kentucky

DIED: April 15, 1865, in Washington, D.C.

BURIED: Oak Ridge Cemetery in Springfield, Illinois

CONTRIBUTION: Self-educated frontiersman who became a successful lawyer; three-time member of the Illinois legislature; member of the U.S. House of Representatives (1846–1849); sixteenth president of the United States (1861–1865). Lincoln led the twenty-three Northern states to victory against the eleven Southern states during the Civil War.

CAUSE OF DEATH: Single gunshot fired from a .44-caliber derringer at point-blank range by distinguished actor and Southern sympathizer John Wilkes Booth while Lincoln was watching the third act of *Our American Cousin* at Ford's Theatre. The bullet entered Lincoln's skull above his left ear, passed through his brain, shattered the orbital plates of both eye sockets, and lodged in the right side of his brain.

JOE LOUIS

BORN: May 13, 1914, near Lafayette, Alabama

DIED: April 12, 1981, in Las Vegas, Nevada

BURIED: Arlington National Cemetery in Arlington, Virginia

CONTRIBUTION: Most devastating boxer in the history of the sport; heavyweight champion of the world for twelve years (1937–1949). He successfully defended his title twenty-five times and won sixty-eight of the seventy-one professional fights in his career. Louis was the first black American to achieve the status of a national hero, and his popularity helped pave the way for other black athletes in professional sports.

CAUSE OF DEATH: Heart attack

JULIETTE GORDON LOW

BORN: October 31, 1860, in Savannah, Georgia

DIED: January 18, 1927, in Savannah, Georgia

BURIED: Laurel Grove Cemetery in Savannah, Georgia

CONTRIBUTION: Organized the first troop of Girl Guides in America on March 12, 1912. The name was changed to Girl Scouts of the United States of America in 1913. Seventeen girls attended the first meeting. Since its origin, more than fifty million young girls have been Girl Scouts.

CAUSE OF DEATH: Breast cancer, which was diagnosed in 1923 and kept secret from her family and friends until shortly before her death. According to her wishes, Low was buried dressed in her Girl Scout uniform.

WILLIAM (BILLY) MANTLE
1957   1994

MICKEY CHARLES MANTLE
1931   1995
A GREAT TEAMMATE

MERLYN LOUISE MANTLE
1932

MICKEY MANTLE

BORN: October 20, 1931, in Spavinaw, Oklahoma

DIED: August 13, 1995, in Dallas, Texas

BURIED: Hillcrest Memorial Park in Dallas, Texas

CONTRIBUTION: Centerfielder and most powerful switch-hitter in baseball history; replaced Joe DiMaggio in 1951 and played for eighteen seasons with the New York Yankees. During his career, Mantle led the American League in home runs four times, played in fourteen All-Star games, and led his team to twelve American League pennants and nine World Series championships. The Yankees retired Mantle's number, seven, in 1969. He was elected to the baseball Hall of Fame in 1974, his first year of eligibility.

CAUSE OF DEATH: Extremely aggressive liver cancer that rapidly spread to his lungs, heart cavity, and other vital organs. He died two months after receiving a liver transplant at Baylor University Medical Center in Dallas.

HENRI MATISSE

BORN: December 31, 1869, in Le Cateau-Cambrésis, France

DIED: November 3, 1954, in Nice, France

BURIED: Cimiez Cemetery in Nice, France

CONTRIBUTION: Innovative French painter, draftsman, sculptor, printmaker, designer, writer, and one of the originators of modern art in the early 1900s. His decorative paintings are characterized by simple designs and rich color.

CAUSE OF DEATH: Heart attack

MARILYN MONROE

BORN: June 1, 1926, in Los Angeles, California

DIED: August 5, 1962, in Los Angeles, California

BURIED: Pierce Brothers Westwood Memorial Park; Los Angeles, California

CONTRIBUTION: Voluptuous and versatile screen actress; gifted comedienne; sex symbol who gained international publicity with her 1949 nude calendar poses; appeared on the cover and inside of the first issue of *Playboy* in December 1953; performed ten shows in four days for 100,000 American troops in Korea in February 1954; appeared in twenty-nine completed films between 1948 and 1962; the most popular and enduring female cultural icon of the twentieth century.

CAUSE OF DEATH: "Acute barbiturate overdose." Suspicious circumstances officially listed Monroe's death as "probable suicide," but compelling evidence and review of postmortem findings suggest that death was not from a self-inflicted or accidental oral overdose, but rather from foul play. Numerous conspiracy and cover-up theories exist. It is likely that Monroe's death was a murder.

RUDOLF NUREYEV

BORN: March 17, 1938, on a train traveling along the shores of Lake Baikal in southeastern Siberia

DIED: January 6, 1993, in Paris, France

BURIED: Cemetery of Ste. Genevieve-des-Bois in Paris, France

CONTRIBUTION: Charismatic, sensual, passionate, and temperamental Russian-born ballet dancer and chore-ographer who studied dance at the Kirov Ballet in Leningrad under Aleksandr Pushkin; defected from the Soviet Union to France on June 17, 1961, and became an Austrian citizen in 1982. Nureyev remained an international star for thirty years, was the director of the Paris Ballet Opera from 1983 to 1989, attracted millions of new fans to ballet, and was a role model for an entire generation of dancers.

CAUSE OF DEATH: AIDS

EDGAR ALLAN POE

BORN: January 19, 1809, in Boston, Massachusetts

DIED: October 7, 1849, in Baltimore, Massachusetts

BURIED: Westminster Burying Ground in Baltimore, Massachusetts

CONTRIBUTION: Literary genius; one of America's greatest literary figures; one of only a few nineteenth-century American writers to receive worldwide acclaim. His imaginative poems and stories often reflected the pain and tragedy of his own life. Poe lived his adult life in poverty and earned little more than $6,000 from his writing.

CAUSE OF DEATH: Suspicious circumstances. Poe was found beaten, robbed, unconscious, and critically ill outside a popular Baltimore tavern. He was brought to a Baltimore hospital on October 6, 1849, and, according to the attending physician, Poe died from encephalitis brought on by exposure.

COLE PORTER

BORN: June 9, 1892, in Peru, Indiana

DIED: October 15, 1964, in Santa Monica, California

BURIED: Mount Hope Cemetery in Peru, Indiana

CONTRIBUTION: Wealthy and charismatic world-famous composer; lyricist of songs for thirty-three stage musicals and numerous films; musical voice of the 1930s Café Society crowd; international celebrity. Porter, who led a sophisticated and opulent lifestyle, composed some of the wittiest, most urbane lyrics and some of the most beautiful music of the twentieth century. He was a legend in his own lifetime. Some of Porter's best-known Broadway shows include *Paris* (1928), *The Gay Divorce* (1932), *Jubilee* (1935), *Kiss Me Kate* (1948), and *Can-Can* (1953). His shows featured such classic songs as "Let's Do It," "Night and Day," "Just One of Those Things," and "I Love Paris."

CAUSE OF DEATH: Complications and infection two days after surgery for removal of kidney stones

COLE PORTER
JUNE 9, 189
OCT. 15, 1964

ELVIS PRESLEY

BORN: January 8, 1935, in East Tupelo, Mississippi

DIED: August 16, 1977, in Memphis, Tennessee

BURIED: Originally buried at Forest Hill Cemetery in Memphis and reinterred in Meditation Gardens on the grounds of Graceland on October 2, 1977

CONTRIBUTION: Self-taught musician and universally proclaimed "King" of rock 'n' roll. Presley's unconventional style, gyrating hips, and baritone voice made him a show-business legend by the age of twenty-five. He recorded 136 gold records, starred in 33 films from 1956 to 1969, gave 1,140 sold-out concerts, and earned an estimated $4.3 billion during his lifetime.

CAUSE OF DEATH: Cardiac arrhythmia. Presley's coronary heart disease, discovered during his autopsy, plus his mild hypertension and long-term dependence and abuse of prescription drugs, contributed to his numerous health problems and death.

PIERRE-AUGUSTE RENOIR

BORN: February 25, 1841, in Limoges, France

DIED: December 3, 1919, in Cages-sur-Mer, France

BURIED: Village Cemetery in Essoyes, France

CONTRIBUTION: French painter, printmaker, and sculptor; one of the originators of the impressionist school of painting; known for his vivid use of color and his paintings of women and landscapes.

CAUSE OF DEATH: Heart attack and pneumonia

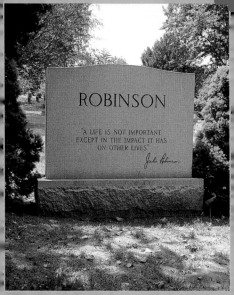

JACKIE ROBINSON

BORN: January 31, 1919, in Cairo, Georgia

DIED: October 24, 1972, in Stamford, Connecticut

BURIED: Cypress Hills Cemetery in Brooklyn, New York

CONTRIBUTION: First African-American to play major league baseball; National League Rookie of the Year (1947); six-time member of National League All Star team; National League MVP (1949); inducted into the Baseball Hall of Fame in 1962. Robinson spent his entire ten-year baseball career as an infielder with the Brooklyn Dodgers and was a symbol for brotherhood and the black man's right to a place in the white community. He was a businessman and civil rights activist after his retirement from baseball.

CAUSE OF DEATH: Heart attack and complications of diabetes after a decade of failing health and two previous heart attacks

ROY ROGERS

BORN: November 5, 1911, in Cincinnati, Ohio

DIED: July 6, 1998, in Apple Valley, California

BURIED: Sunset Hills Memorial Park in Apple Valley, California

CONTRIBUTION: Quintessential ever-honest "King of the Cowboys." He always played the good guy as a singer and actor in eighty-seven musical westerns and 101 half-hour TV shows. At the peak of his popularity, in the decade after the end of World War II, more than four hundred Roy Rogers licensed products were available in the Sears catalog; Roy Rogers comic books sold twenty-five million copies per year; and his radio show was broadcast on more than five hundred stations.

CAUSE OF DEATH: Congestive heart failure

NOTE: His given name was Leonard Franklin Slye. The name was legally changed to Roy Rogers in 1942.

Roy Rogers

33

Leonard Franklin Slye
Nov. 5, 1911 — July 6, 1998

"MAY
THE DIVINE SPIRIT
THAT ANIMATED
BABE RUTH
TO WIN THE CRUCIAL
GAME OF LIFE
INSPIRE THE YOUTH
OF AMERICA"
CARDINAL SPELLMAN

GEORGE HERMAN RUTH
1895 – 1948
CLAIRE RUTH

RUTH

GEORGE HERMAN "BABE" RUTH

BORN: February 6, 1895, in Baltimore, Maryland

DIED: August 16, 1948, in New York, New York

BURIED: Gate of Heaven Cemetery in Valhallah, New York

CONTRIBUTION: Baseball's greatest star, most enduring legend, and idol of children. Ruth's major league career spanned twenty-two seasons (the Boston Red Sox from 1914 to 1920, the New York Yankees from 1920 to 1934, and the Boston Braves in 1934). At the time of his death, Ruth held fifty-four major league records. In 1936 he was one of the first five men elected to the National Baseball Hall of Fame. The total salary he earned as a professional baseball player was $910,900.

CAUSE OF DEATH: Throat cancer and pulmonary complications

COLONEL HARLAND SANDERS

BORN: September 9, 1890, in Henryville, Kentucky

DIED: December 16, 1980, in Shelbyville, Kentucky

BURIED: Cave Hill Cemetery in Louisville, Kentucky

CONTRIBUTION: Seventh-grade dropout who opened Sander's Cafe in the rear of a service station in 1929. His specially seasoned fried chicken, prepared in a pressure cooker, was so successful that Sanders eventually sold franchises and established the Kentucky Fried Chicken Corporation. By 1963 there were six hundred outlets. In 1964 Sanders sold his business for $2 million but remained as an adviser, publicist, and board member of the company.

CAUSE OF DEATH: Acute stem-cell leukemia and pneumonia

FRANK SINATRA

BORN: December 12, 1915, in Hoboken, New Jersey

DIED: May 14, 1998, in Los Angeles, California

BURIED: Desert Memorial Park in Cathedral City, California

CONTRIBUTION: Master interpreter of lyrics; charismatic balladeer of sentimental love songs; teen idol of the 1940s and first modern superstar; Academy Award–winning actor and star of more than fifty films; multiple Grammy Award winner; television star; artist; businessman; philanthropist. He dominated popular music longer than any entertainer in history and will be remembered as one of the greatest cultural icons of the twentieth century.

CAUSE OF DEATH: Heart attack

HENRY DAVID THOREAU

BORN: July 12, 1817, in Concord, Massachusetts

DIED: May 6, 1862, in Concord, Massachusetts

BURIED: Sleepy Hollow Cemetery in Concord, Massachusetts, on "Authors' Ridge," close to the graves of his friends Ralph Waldo Emerson, Louisa May Alcott, and Nathaniel Hawthorne

CONTRIBUTION: Major nineteenth-century essayist; naturalist; social critic; writer; major figure in the transcendentalist movement who placed nature above materialism and ethics above conformity. Best known for his two-year experiment of living a simple life in the cabin he built on the shores of Ralph Waldo Emerson's property at Walden Pond. Thoreau's most famous works include "Civil Disobedience" (1849), his essay about passive resistance that influenced the philosophy of Martin Luther King Jr., and *Walden, or, Life in the Woods* (1854).

CAUSE OF DEATH: A cold that developed into bronchitis and induced a recurrence of Thoreau's tuberculosis

JOHN THOREAU
Born Oct. 8, 1787. Died Feb. 3, 1859.

CYNTHIA D. his wife
Born 1787. Died 1872

JOHN THOREAU JR.
1815. Died 1842

HELEN L. THOREAU

HENRY D. THOREAU

SOPHIA E. THOREAU

THOREAU

FATHER

MOTHER

MARK TWAIN

BORN: November 30, 1835, in Hannibal, Missouri

DIED: April 3, 1910, in Redding, Connecticut

BURIED: Woodlawn Cemetery in Elmira, New York

CONTRIBUTION: Onetime Mississippi River steamboat pilot who became a legendary American novelist, lecturer, satirist, student of human nature, storyteller, and the greatest humorist of his age. Considered the "Dean of American Literature," Twain won worldwide acclaim for his stories about youthful adventures. He is best known for *The Adventures of Tom Sawyer* (1876), *A Tramp Abroad* (1880), and *The Adventure of Huckleberry Finn* (1884).

CAUSE OF DEATH: Angina pectoris one week after returning from a three-month stay in Bermuda where he went to recuperate for his failing health and broken heart following the accidental drowning death of his youngest daughter on Christmas Eve, 1909

VINCENT VAN GOGH

BORN: March 30, 1853, in Groot-Zundert, Holland

DIED: July 29, 1890, in Auvers-sur-Oise, France

BURIED: Auvers-sur-Oise Cemetery in Auvers-sur-Oise, France

CONTRIBUTION: Onetime art dealer, teacher, and missionary who was active as an artist for the last ten years of his life. Van Gogh was unknown as an artist and sold only one painting during his lifetime. He was supported financially by his brother and won adulation and respect only after his death. He is considered the greatest Dutch painter after Rembrandt and the most widely influential of the post-impressionist painters. Ravaged by rejection, disappointment, and mental illness, van Gogh spent twelve months in an asylum and was released just two months before he committed suicide.

CAUSE OF DEATH: Self-inflicted gunshot wound to the chest on July 27, 1890, in a field outside of Auvers-sur-Oise. Badly wounded, van Gogh returned to his residence at a local inn, the Auberge Ravoux, where he died two days later.

JULES VERNE

BORN: February 8, 1828, in Nantes, France

DIED: March 24, 1905, in Amiens, France

BURIED: Cimitière de la Madeline in Amiens, France

CONTRIBUTION: Former stockbroker and imaginative nineteenth-century writer of futuristic novels such as *From the Earth to the Moon* (1865), *20,000 Leagues Under the Sea* (1870), and *Around the World in Eighty Days* (1873). In these and other novels, Verne accurately predicted many of the technological advances of the twentieth century. He is regarded as the father of science fiction and was an inspiration to many future explorers, inventors, and scientists.

CAUSE OF DEATH: Diabetes

GEORGE WASHINGTON

BORN: February 22, 1732, at Popes Creek Plantation in Westmoreland County, Virginia

DIED: December 14, 1799, in Mt. Vernon, Virginia

BURIED: Mt. Vernon, Virginia

CONTRIBUTION: Virginia surveyor; farmer and plantation owner; member of the Virginia militia in 1750s; commander-in-chief of the Continental Army (1775–1783); president of the Constitutional Convention in 1787; first president of the United States. During his two terms in office, Washington set up five executive departments (state, treasury, war, attorney general, and postmaster); established a banking system, a system of taxation, and a federal court system; and kept the nation at peace.

CAUSE OF DEATH: Streptococcus infection and swelling of the throat following a severe cold

FRANK LLOYD WRIGHT

BORN: June 8, 1867, in Richland, Wisconsin

DIED: April 9, 1959, in Phoenix, Arizona

BURIED: Taliesin West in Scottsdale, Arizona*

OCCUPATION: Flamboyant, eccentric, arrogant, imaginative, and controversial architectural genius who led a tempestuous, scandalous, and extravagant personal life and who is considered by many to have been the greatest and most influential architect of the twentieth century. His "organic" style of architecture emphasized the correlation and harmony between buildings and nature. Throughout his seventy-year career, Wright designed more than four hundred structures including well-known residences, office and government buildings, museums, hotels, schools, exposition halls, banks, churches, and synagogues.

CAUSE OF DEATH: Complications following emergency surgery on April 4, 1959, for removal of an intestinal obstruction

* This photograph is of Wright's original grave site in a family burial ground at the cemetery at Unity Chapel in Spring Green, Wisconsin, where he was buried on April 12, 1959. In accordance with the will of his third wife, Oligvanna, Wright's remains were exhumed on March 25, 1985, cremated, and sent to Taliesin West where his ashes were interred in a memorial wall next to those of his wife.